MW01288767

Build a Kindle Edition Anyone Can!

Build a Kindle Edition— Anyone Can!

How to Create and Publish Your eBook

By J.M. LaRoche

Published by

HTMPulishing

htmpublishing.net

In memory of
Benjamin Franklin's
contributions to Democracy

Acknowledgements

A big "thank you" for advice, inspiration, products, or services to the following: the folks at Kindle Korner, Joe Wikert, Bartleby, Library of Congress, Project Gutenberg, U.S. Archives and Records Administration, Wikipedia and Wikimedia Commons, GIMP, Notepad++, Scintilla.org for SciTE, OpenOffice.org, Ron Burkey for GutenMark, Virdi Software for Text2HTML, Yahoo! GeoCities, and Google for Blogger & Picasa. Of course, a really big "THANK YOU" to Amazon.com.

Image of Benjamin Franklin's printing press from *Historic Tales* by Charles Morris.

About the Author

I have been involved in helping other content creators through editing, book layout, graphics, cover design, publication, and promotion of content for eBooks and print-on-demand books. Since the arrival of the Kindle, my primary focus is the production of books according to the Amazon's particular requirements for Kindle Editions.

I have authored two published works of nonfiction prior to this book. One is viewable at Google Book Search. There, adventurous cooks can help themselves to "Cultivated Recipes for Uncultivated Foods" in *Wild Fare*.

Comments, suggestions, and notification of errors about this book are welcome at
the blog "Build a Kindle Edition"
http://buildakindleedition.blogspot.com.

For assistance in preparing your eBook,
contact jameslaroche@htmpublishing.net.

Contents

1
Anyone
Can Build a Kindle Edition

DANA, MY NEIGHBOR, owns a Kindle. One afternoon in my neighbor's backyard, I chatted with Dana about the Kindle's features. Dana's mom was sitting with us at the picnic table on a beautiful bright cloudless day. Mom had ordered the present for the Holiday Season. She takes pride in seeing that Dana is well equipped for college. Here's a reconstruction of the conversation between me, Jim (J), Dana (D), and Mom (M).

J: Dana, I've noticed you with your Kindle in your yard chair from time to time.

D: I really enjoy kicking my feet up and lounging back in the fresh air with a good read. Reading an eBook with my Kindle sure beats having to lug my old laptop out. Its battery doesn't hold a charge for long. Now, I don't have to worry about that, or being tethered to an electrical outlet. I used to find it hard to get into a book's story on the laptop. Now, with the Kindle, I'm absorbed in the book in no time. I just hardly seem to be aware of the hardware.

J: What are you reading today?

D: I'm almost finished with *Team of Rivals: The Political Genius of Abraham Lincoln* by Doris Kearns Goodwin. My birthday was last month. If anyone hinted about what kind of present I'd like, I would reply, "an Amazon Gift Card, please!" So, I got a bunch of Kindle Editions. 'Got one for Mom, too.

M: That was nice of you, Dana. And, I'm really enjoying it. I was feeling guilty about using your Kindle so much to read it. So, I just ordered a new Kindle just for myself ... well, for me *and* Dad.

J: Dana, I read that book in hardcover when it was first published. I found it to be a fascinating historical study. Your college major is History, right?

D: Right! I received my undergrad degree this year, and I'm accepted for a masters program starting in the Fall.

M: That's my Dana. The apple doesn't fall far from the tree!

D: Jim, Mom's right. You know, she's a member of the research board of our local historical society. She is a strong influence.

J: Dana, do you have reading material other than books on your Kindle?

D: A few blogs and newspapers, and I use Amazon's conversion service to store a lot of my class notes and essay assignments. In fact, with all the papers I have written for different courses, my list is starting to look a little long and cluttered.

J: You know, you could compile your papers with a table of contents and have a customized Kindle Edition for your personal use.

D: Wow! I like that. I could group all the papers I wrote about the American Revolution together in one edition. Oooh! ... but, how would I do it?

J: At my job, I've been publishing Kindle Editions since Amazon introduced their eReader. I could show you how.

Mom: I've been thinking about the documents I have gathered for the Historical Society. I think there might be a lot of people interested in our region's past who could benefit from a published collection.

J: You have a couple of great ideas for Kindle Editions—one for Dana's personal book, and one that you, Mom, could offer in the Kindle Store.

That conversation was the genesis of this book.

I have been involved with authors who dreamed of having their manuscripts in book form. Approaching large publishing houses, or finding an agent can be daunting. Print-on-demand paper books and eBooks in PDF format started to open wide the gates to publication for many writers.

When Amazon followed Sony's lead in offering an eReader with a paper-like E Ink display it satisfied a need of readers. Amazon took a giant step farther in satisfying the needs of authors by opening its Digital Text Platform (DTP) to all. The Open Source movement unleashed programming creativity. I believe it will be rivaled by what I call the paradigm of "Open Publishing" that Amazon encourages through DTP. No agents needed, no ISBN's needed. The only thing that is needed is what readers want and authors provide.

As Amazon states in large letters on its front page at **dtp.amazon.com**, "Welcome...Its Your Thing...Do It...Your Way."

Welcome to Digital Text Platform

Digital Text Platform is a fast and easy self-publishing tool that lets you upload and format your books for sale in the Kindle Store.

It's Your Thing. Have a book you want to sell? Sign up with Digital Text Platform and publish your content in the Amazon Kindle Store in minutes.

Do It. If you have an Amazon.com account, you're already signed up with Digital Text Platform. Start publishing now!

Your Way. Digital Text Platform gives you everything you need to become your own publisher today. See for yourself.

Amazon.com Digital Text Platform Welcome

Now is an historic time. Publishing has been democratized. Others see it. Google Book Search has dropped its former requirement for ISBNs.

Mr. Bezos and company carry forward the torch that a past American genius and luminary lit.

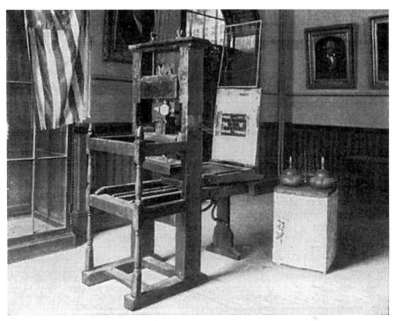

Franklin's Printing Press

2
Book Content

Creating New Content | Re-using Content
Planning Content

BOOKS WRITTEN in narrative style, fiction or nonfiction, are well suited as Kindle Editions. Generally, works of fiction are easy to publish as Kindle Editions. Difficulties arise when content is in columns or in tables. Content in a table layout must be modified to present the content linearly or be converted to an image like the one below.

	1875	1880	1886	
	s. d.	s. d	s. d.	
Bremen, 1867, 5 sgr., green, *unused*	1 0	1 6	2 6	
Bechuanaland, 1886, 1s., *used*	—	—	—	
" 1888-9, 4d., *unused*	—	—	—	

Table Example

The reason is that Kindle users can adjust the size of text displayed. When a reader increases the text size, the content must be free to flow along the screen width. For that reason, complex layouts, such as text constricted in multiple columns, as in print newspapers, won't work.

IS bad enough to have people who have reached years
f discretion use "patent
clues" recklessly; still, if
come to grief it is their own
r—unless all the blame may
likly charged to the manu-
rers. But what about the
ts? Whose fault if they
r?
ow many parents ever stop
unk whether there may be

Thirteen Little Victims of
Man's Greed

JERY ROGERS
2 years, 8 months old
Died in April, 1904
Buffalo, New York.

ADAM and EVE GNAB
1 month old
Died in January, 1900
Utica, New York.

MENTION has been ma
three deaths in Cleve
due to the use of one kic
medicine, but that is not the
one that has proved dis
ous in that city. Last sur
a doctor was called to atte
a girl eight months old who
been restless all night. Qu
his experienced eyes det
evidence of the use of
opiate. The parents, b

Columns Example

Creating New Content

When I type a plan for a book, research notes, or start
drafting book content, I often use Microsoft Notepad or
another brand of text editor. Notepad is a great "bare
bones" program with a good set of basic features. It is
included with every copy of Windows, and by default
.txt documents open in Notepad. I also use SciTE which
has more "bells and whistles" and can be more useful for
other types of projects.

Creating Text

Most use WYSIWYG programs (what you see is what
you get), e.g. Microsoft Word, to type documents. Word
and similar composers relieve users from hand-coding.
They enable quick insertion of document elements like
links, images, and headings without any knowledge of
HyperText Markup Language (HTML).

When starting a book "from scratch", I prefer a simple
text editor to a WYSIWYG editor because I can type
HTML directly. I have direct control over the document.
To have that level of control for creating Kindle Editions
requires knowing some HTML. Some folks object to the
requirement of learning markup language until they
learn that there are only about two-dozen new terms
(tags) they have to learn. From my experience, just about

anyone can learn to hand-code HTML in an hour. That's it... about two-dozen new items to memorize and 1 hour of practice—it's not rocket science! There is a list of HTML tags and attribute-value pairs supported by Kindle in Chapter 10 "Kindle HTML Tags". The most frequently used tags account for about half of those in that list. The next chapter includes a mini tutorial "Quick & Easy HTML" that lists the tags to memorize and tips to help practice.

Creating Images
Creating images for your book project is easy. For non-digital camera photos, film can be processed to digital images at facilities that develop film. Photography stores can scan photos previously developed onto paper prints into digital images. Of course, if you have a digital camera you can directly upload your images to your computer or an online album service like Google's Picasa Web Albums. Google offers the Picasa image editor as a free download to install on your computer. Picasa has a good set of features for editing your digital images.

Book cover images for eBooks sold in the Kindle Store are discussed in the next chapter in the section titled "Cover Images".

Re-using Content

Dana wants to compile some papers composed in Word for a college course into a personal eBook. Dana will create an eBook of several chapters, each consisting of one of the academic papers, and with each chapter linked to a table of contents. Dana will have the finished .html book made into an .azw book through Amazon's conversion service. Dana can provide no-cost copies of the book by sending it to any someone@kindle.com.

Mom has documents from the Historical Society publications in Microsoft Word .doc format, and pages from the organization's Web site in .html format. She has research notes in .txt format, and illustrations and photos from Nineteenth-century publications as developed prints, transparency slides, and digital images in .jpg format. She has researched the sources of the old documents to be sure they are in the public domain since she plans to publish her compilation for sale in the Kindle Store. How to convert text content from different formats is covered in Chapter 3.

Mom created a list of some sources of content that might be at hand for others interested in family history:
- diaries and journals
- civil and religious records
- documents and promotional materials from a family-owned business
- personal correspondence
- scrapbooks
- genealogical research notes and documents

I have found it convenient for my personal use to create custom travel guides. The Kindle is a great convenience when travelling for business or pleasure. I compile my itinerary along with my notes and maps about the destination's attractions that I'm interested in. Here is a sample list of contents from a personal eBook that I built for a recent business trip:
- Schedule for Trip
- Conference Center and Hotel Maps

- Conference Exhibition Floor Plan
- Tourist Attractions with Maps
- Miscellaneous To-Do List

There are many Web sites that host public domain content that can be helpful for book projects. Be cautious and check at each site regarding policies and rights to copying and distribution.

The National Archives and Records Administration (NARA) states:
"Generally, materials produced by Federal agencies are in the public domain and may be reproduced without permission. However, not all materials appearing on this web site are in the public domain. Some materials have been donated or obtained from individuals or organizations and may be subject to restrictions on use, where cited. Please note that because we cannot guaranty the status of specific items, you use materials found in our holdings at your own risk.

Images on our web site which are in the public domain may be used without permission. If you use images from NARA's holdings, we ask that you credit NARA as the source. Please note that some images on our site have been obtained from other organizations. Permission to use these images should be obtained directly from those organizations."
— www.ourdocuments.gov/content.php?page=privacy

Project Gutenberg states:
"Public Domain Books
These books are in the public domain in the United States and everybody — including Project Gutenberg and

you—may read and distribute them. If you don't live in the United States you'll have to check the laws of the country you live in before downloading and distributing our ebooks.

A Project Gutenberg ebook is made out of two parts: the public domain book and the non public domain Project Gutenberg trademark and license. If you strip the Project Gutenberg license and all references to Project Gutenberg from the ebook, you are left with a public domain ebook. You can do anything you want with that."
—www.gutenberg.org/wiki/Main_Page. Click for License and Trademark information.

Planning Content

I like to write a plan for my writing projects even if its just a basic outline of the scope of the project. It helps me to focus. Its not a static document. I update it when I scale the project up or down. If you are collaborating with another writer, this can be helpful as a single shared reference for project coordination. Noted updates will provide a change log.

I have packaged a downloadable set of lists and tenplates that can help in bookbuilding projects. Go to the download page for Builders_Kit.zip (geocities.com/jameslaroche).

Bookbuilders_Kit.zip includes READ_ME_FIRST.html (this file) and
KIT.txt
Kindle_HTML_Tags_Sampler.zip

Checklist_for_Commercial_Kindle_Editions.html
Checklist_for_Noncommercial_Kindle_Editions.html
Template_for_Book_Plan.html
Template_for_Publishing_Plan.html
Template_for_Tag_Skeleton-Fiction.html
Template_for_Tag Skeleton-Nonfiction.html

KIT.txt can be useful in saving time by copying tags from it and pasting them in your project as needed.
Kindle HTML Tags Sampler.zip can be uploaded to DTP to demonstrate in Preview how the tags will show in Kindle. Sign in to DTP, click "Add item" Enter "Kindle HTML Tags Sampler" or any other title name you like, fill in the other required fields, "Save," and "Upload" so you can view the file in Preview.
For the remaining files:
Create a folder for your Kindle Edition project in your computer's file directory.
Copy these files to your project folder.
Rename copy of Template_for_Book_Plan.html, as TITLE_Book_Plan.html.
Replace capitalized words with your info.
Rename copy of Template_for_Publishing_Plan.html as TITLE_Publishing_Plan.html,
Open the renamed files in a text editor and modify with your info.
Choose a Tag Skeleton template to copy.
Rename the copy of the skeleton as TITLE.html
Open TITLE.html in your text editor.
Edit the capitalized words with your info and add your book's body content.

The Template_for_Tag_Skeleton-Fiction.html is useful for books that *do not require* a Table of Contents or page breaks after the title page.

Tip: Kindle owners may sample 10% of a book. If your book is 10 pages or smaller, do not have a page break after the title page so customers can sample some of your content.

The Template_for_Tag Skeleton-Nonfiction.html is useful for books that require a Table of Contents and section page breaks after the title page.

In the chapter section, there is sample code "<img src="NAME.EXT">" for including images.

Delete or add sections according to your book's needs.

The following is a template of a basic book plan that I use.

Template—Book Plan

* Replace capitalized words with your info.

Book Genre

GENRE (e.g. Historical Fiction)
KINDLE CATEGORY (DTP accepts 5 maximum, e.g. Kindle Books > Fiction > Historical Fiction)

Book Topic

TOPIC (e.g. a Militia recruit meets Franklin in Philadelphia.)

Readership

READERSHIP (e.g. Personal (not for sale), General Public, Young Adults, Professionals, etc.)

Text Length

PAGES (e.g. 250 pages)

Research Time

TIME (e.g. 2 weeks)

Writing Time

TIME (e.g. 50 days, 250 pages divided by 5 pages per day)

Here's the plan I used for this book. You can see a change where an original entry has been struck through followed by its replacement.

Build a Kindle Edition Book Plan

Book Genre
Kindle Books > Nonfiction > General
Kindle Books > Business & Investing > General
Kindle Books > Computers & Internet > Hardware
Kindle Books > Reference Publishing & Books > Authorship
Kindle Books > Nonfiction > Reference > Writing

Book Topic
Creating, publishing, and promoting Kindle Editions

Readership
General Public

Text Length
100 to 125 pp.

Planning & Research
~~1 week, create book plan with chapters' topics outline on book building with one example Kindle Edition, target 8/28~~ [changed 8/24]
2 weeks, create outline on book building with three example Kindle Editions, target 9/4

Writing Time
125 pages divided by 5pp/day = 24 days

November 2007, Kindle eReader introduced by Amazon.com

Summary

- Start your project with a written book plan.

- Use a simple text editor like Notepad, Notepad++, or SciTE to create content. See Chapter 9 "Online Resources" Editing Software.
- Take control—tag it yourself! See Chapter 2 "Book Building" Quick & Easy HTML, and Chapter 10 "Kindle HTML Tags".
- Create new content. See Chapter 9 "Online Resources" Aids for Writing.
- Re-use content. See Chapter 9 "Online Resources" Public Domain Content.

Next, we'll move on to the core of this book. The next chapter, "Book Building", is "where the rubber meets the road."

3
Book Building

Text | Quick & Easy HTML
Images in Books | Cover Images

J: We'll start with a written organization plan for the book project.

D: OK, just like having a written book plan, we have a written a plan for making the book.

J: Exactly! Here's a list of steps that we'll follow.

First, we download Bookbuilders_Kit.zip and extract its files.
The package includes:
READ_ME_FIRST.html
KIT.txt
Kindle_HTML_Tags_Sampler.zip
Checklist_for_Commercial_Kindle_Editions.html
Checklist_for_Noncommercial_Kindle_Editions.html
Template_for_Book_Plan.html
Template_for_Publishing_Plan.html
Template_for_Tag_Skeleton-Fiction.html
Template_for_Tag Skeleton-Nonfiction.html

Next, in our browser we open "Checklist for Noncommercial Kindle Edition." That is the organization plan for the book project. Below is a copy of it:

Checklist for Noncommercial Kindle Editions

Note: capitalized words are stand-ins for your names.

1. Folder Setup

In a computer's My Documents folder, create a new folder named KEP or whatever name you like. I use KEP as the abbreviation for Kindle Edition Project. If you are building several books, consider a folder hierarchy like My Documents/KEP/KEP TITLE-1/.
Create a sub folder named "images", or whatever you like, if there are images in the book's text.
Create a sub folder named "docs", or whatever you like, and move the extracted files from Bookbuilders_Kit.zip to it.
Go to My Documents/KEB/KEB TITLE-1/docs/ and rename Template_for_Book_Plan.html to TITLE_Book_Plan.html.
Rename the appropriate tag skeleton template to TITLE.html

2. Tools Setup

Run your browser.
Run your text editor.
Run your spell checker.

3. Book Building

In your browser open:
My Documents/KEP/KEP TITLE-1/docs/
Bookbuilding_List_for_Noncommercial_Kindle_Editions.html
(this list),
My Documents/KEP/KEP TITLE-1/TITLE.html, and
My Documents/KEP/KEP
TITLE-1TITLE_Book_Plan.html.
In your browsers Bookmarks create a folder KEP and
bookmark the above files so you can open them
individually or as a group.

In your text editor, open:
My Documents/KEP/KEP TITLE-1/TITLE.html and
My Documents/KEP/KEP
TITLE-1TITLE_Book_Plan.html.
Modify both as needed.

4. Proofreading

After adding your content to the tag skeleton and
building the book's front matter:
in your spell checker, check My Documents/KEP/KEP
TITLE-1/TITLE.html for misspellings and grammatical
errors.
in your browser, proofread My Documents/KEP/KEP
TITLE-1/TITLE.html checking layout, punctuation, and
syntax.
in your browser, validate the file's HTML code.

5. Package and Send

Zip up My Documents/KEP/KEP TITLE-1/TITLE.html. If there are images, add images/ to TITLE.zip.
eMail TITLE.zip to USER-ID@kindle.com

For a book that will be offered in the Kindle store, step 5 is changed to:

5. Publishing

Zip up My Documents/KEP/KEP TITLE-1/TITLE.html. If there are images, add images/ to TITLE.zip.
Create TITLE_cover.jpg.
Create a blurb and "Save As" TITLE_Blurb.txt (4,000 characters maximum).
Create TITLE_Keywords.txt , add a list of keywords appropriate to your book's content, the more the better, aim for a dozen.
Sign in at DTP, click "Add new item".
1. Enter Product Details:
fill in Title,
fill in Description copying Blurb.txt,
add Publisher and date,
select Categories,
fill in Authors,
fill in Search Keywords copying Keywords.txt,
upload Product Image (TITLE_cover.jpg),
Save entries.
2. Upload and Preview Book:
upload TITLE.zip & proofread the book in Preview Mode.
3. Enter Price:

fill in price and Save.

Click "Publish".

DTP will display "Publishing [TITLE].Your content is being published. It will be live in 12 to 72 hours." Visit Amazon's Kindle Store (amazon.com/kindle) in 12 to 72 hours to search for the catalog listing of your title. Proofread your entries (title, author, publisher, etc.) in the book's product page. Your description will be added to the product page in 3 to 10 working days. Proofread the description when it is added.

After opening Book Plan, Checklist, and Tag Skeleton in your browser, bookmark them so you can quickly set up everything you need for further writing/editing sessions.

Session Bookmarks
Create a bookmark folder named for your project.
Bookmark your project checklist (either for Commercial Kindle Editions or for Noncommercial Kindle Editions).
Bookmark your book plan.
Bookmark TITLE.html.
Bookmark http://dtp.amazon.com.
(If you use an online file storage service to backup your files, bookmark that too.)

In Firefox, when your mouse cursor is at your Bookmarks project folder, right click and Open All in Tabs.

Let' start building a Kindle Edition. Select TITLE.html from your browser tabs. Change all tag skeleton capitalized placers to your words. We are ready to add content to the template.

Text

Content from .html

Text already formatted in HTML is the easiest to use for your projects. Any text styling such as bold or italic text has already been added, as well as link tags, image tags, heading tags, etc. To build a book with an HTML file, open the .html file in Notepad, place your mouse cursor at the beginning of the text that you want to add to your template, click and drag to highlight to the end of your content, then copy (right click - Copy, or Ctrl+C). Paste your copied text into the template and Save. Other free text editors are listed in Chapter 9 "Online Resources" Editing Software.

When re-using content that is formatted in HTML, check for tags that are not supported in the Kindle. The use of Search in a text editor to Find "<table" and "<pre" will locate sections where a browser screen shot image could substitute for the tabled or preformatted text.

If you are working from an .html file that has links referencing page numbers, you may want to eliminate them from your Kindle Edition. The original version's page numbers may not correspond to Kindle pages, particularly when readers adjust text size. An easy way to delete page references is by using the editor's Search > Find feature. Find the files page references, then Replace the reference with the same wording **except** add "<!--" to the beginning of the wording. Find again and Replace the

wording with "-->" added to the end of the wording. You have now commented-out all internal page references. Find and Replace is a simple, powerful technique that can be a time saver for many similar chores.

Content from .txt
If your text is from a .txt file you will have to add HTML tags to create double line spaces between paragraphs. The quickest way to do that is with a text to HTML conversion program. See Chapter 9 "Online Resources" Editing Software for Text2Web, a free program that will create a new .html file with your source .txt file content converted to unindented paragraphs.

Text2Web does one thing—it converts text file paragraphs to unindented HTML file paragraphs. Any additional HTML features, e.g. link tags, image tags, heading tags, etc., have to be added. Note that Text2Web will preserve vertical white space. That can be an advantage when you do not have sections in the book body separated by page breaks. The vertical spacing will indicate a section break to the reader

Another .txt to .html converter is GutenMark. This converter was designed to handle the peculiarities of Project Gutenberg text files. It converts text file paragraphs to indented HTML paragraphs and will convert Gutenberg marks for italics to HTML tagged italics. It has a check box labelled "Split at headings?" in its lower Settings section. If that box is checked, the program will generate a linked Table of Contents for the converted file. See Chapter 9 "Online Resources" Editing Software for a link to this free program.

Content from .doc & .rtf,

Word files, .doc & .rtf, can be converted to .html via OpenOffice.org's Writer. Open the Word file in Writer and Save As .html.

Content from .pdf

If you are working from a PDF file that permits its content to be copied to your clipboard, create a new file in Notepad and paste from .pdf to .txt. Then convert from .txt to .html.

It's time for a crash course in HyperText Markup.

Quick & Easy HTML

The Kindle uses a simplified set of official HTML tags. Of the complete official HTML set, Kindle Editions need less than half . And, of those tags that Kindle supports, less than half again, are needed for the average document.

HTML documents consist of: document structure elements,
page block-level elements—such as headings, paragraphs, divisions, and lists, which can include images and text.
tags—paired, or open, which can include attribute-value pairs.
Tags must be *nested correctly*. Example of incorrect nesting: nested incorrectly
Special Character Entities can be included with the appropriate character code number.

For a complete HTML tutorial visit W3Schools.com.

For advice from experienced Kindle Edition publishers visit Amazon Digital Platform's Community Support Forums.

Document Structure
<html> </html> All Kindle HTML files must include these.
<body> </body> All Kindle HTML files must include these.

Page Elements
<mbp:pagebreak /> This is not an official HTML tag. It is a custom Kindle/Mobipocket tag.
<p> </p> double spaces paragraphs with first paragraph line indented.
<div> </div> double space before and after content within the "division".

 for a line break , <hr> for a horizontal rule, <img> for an image. Note that these three tags do not use end tags, e.g.
 </br> is invalid.

Create a Basic Page
Use Microsoft Notepad or other text editor to make a quick template that will be copied to save time in creating future HTML files. To find Notepad click your computer's left bottom 'start', scroll to 'programs' then to 'accessories'. The template will have a minimal tag set—just enough to display the document. There are just three steps to follow:
1. Type <html></html>.
2. Move your cursor between the 'html' start and end tags, then type <body></body>.
3. Move your cursor between the 'body' start and end

tags, then type <h1></h1> and add the temporary placer word TITLE between the level-1 heading tags. Now you have

<html><body><h1>TITLE</h1></body></html>.

It's good to think in tag sets, i.e. you must have a pair of tags—start tag plus end tag (end tags have a slash) for each tag type—except three tags that will discuss soon. That's the minimum tag set needed to display your eBook. Now, let's organize the tags in a traditional vertical arrangement. Let's refer to this as a tag set skeleton. Double space between the heading tags to reserve space for the meat of the body—your future book content.

```
<html>
<body>
<h1>TITLE</h1>

</body>
</html>
```

Now "Save As" template-tag-skeleton.html or some other name meaningful to you. Open the template file in your browser and proofread it. By the way, you'll be seeing that phrase "proofread it' frequently— it's a quality control step that should become second nature at every major phase of of the project.

The Bookbuilders' Kit includes a list of "Most Frequently Used HTML Tags for Kindle Editions":

Kindle's Important HTML Tags (KIT)
or
The Most Frequently Used HTML Tags for Kindle
Editions

This file can be useful in saving time by copying tags
from here and pasting them in your project as needed.

*Change capitalized items to your values.

1 HTML <html> </html>
2 Body <body> </body>
3 Headings:
Largest <h1> </h1>
2nd largest <h2> </h2>
3rd largest <h3> </h3>
4th largest <h4> </h4>
4 Paragraphs <p> </p>
5 Line Break
6 Center for text <center> </center>
7 Horizontal Rule Line <hr>
8 Division <div> </div>
to center an image use:

<div align="center">
<img src="XYZ">
CAPTION
</div>

9 Lists:
ordered (numbered) list <ol> </ol>
unordered (bullet) list <ul> </ul>
list item <li> </li>

10 Image <img src="XYZ">
11 Link Anchor <a href="XYZ"> </a>
12 Bold <b> </b>
13 Italic <i> </i>
14 Font <font size="N"> </font>

For demonstrations of the tags' effects, see
Kindle_HTML_Tags_Sampler.zip

Kindle HTML Tags Sampler

*"a decorative piece of needlework typically having letters or verses embroidered on it in various stitches as an example..." —Merriam-Webster

Heading Tags Demo

<h1></h1> for

Level 1 Heading

<h2></h2> for

Level 2 Heading

<h3></h3> for

Level 3 Heading

<h4></h4> for

Level 4 Heading

<h4 align="center">Centered Example</h4>

<h4 align="center">Right Margin Example</h4>

<h5></h5> for

Level 5 Heading

<h6></h6> for

Level 6 Heading

Paragraph Tags Demo

By default, paragraph text is displayed with full justified alignment, and automatic hyphenation. The first line of each paragraph is automatically indented. Readers can adjust the alignment in the Kindle. If you need to override the user-adjustable indentation, use any of the following:
align="left" forces an unindented paragraph.

 forces an unindented paragraph..

 div align="left" forces an unindented paragraph.

Alter first line paragraph indentation by using the width

attribute:
<p width="N"> (pixels), <p width="N%"> (percent of page width), <p width="Nem"> (width of letter "M"), or <p width="Npt"> (points).
Examples:
<p width="0"> No indent.</p>
<p width="10%"> Indent (10% of page width)</p>
<p width="5em"> Indent (5 em).</p>

Line Break Tag Demo

 Creates a line break. This is an open tag (not paired, i.e. there is no such tag as </br>).

Center Tag for Text Demo

<center> </center> Centers text horizontally, e.g.
<center>Page Center</center>

Horizontal Rule Line Demo

<hr> Horizontal rule line to divide sections. This is an open tag, i.e. not paired.
It accepts the attribute-value pair width="N" (N may be a number or %),

<hr color="gray" >:

Division Tag Demo

Division <div> </div> defines a division or section of a document.
It accepts the attribute-value pair align="left", e.g.
this division is at **left margin**.
or the attribute-value pair align="center", e.g.
this division is at **center** page.
or the attribute-value pair align="right", e.g.
this division is at **right margin**.
To center an image use:

<div align="center">
<img src="XYZ">
CAPTION
</div>

Lorem ipsum dolor sit amet, consectetur adipisicing elit, sed do eiusmod tempor incididunt ut labore et dolore magna aliqua. Ut enim ad minim veniam, quis nostrud exercitation ullamco laboris nisi ut aliquip ex ea commodo consequat.

America's Historic Documents

Duis aute irure dolor in reprehenderit in voluptate velit esse cillum dolore eu fugiat nulla pariatur. Excepteur sint occaecat cupidatat non proident, sunt in culpa qui officia deserunt mollit anim id est laborum.

Lists Tags Demo

<dl> </dl> Creates a definition list of enclosed definitions <dd> </dd> each followed by an enclosed definition term <dt> </dt>. Note <dd> is indented.
<dl>
<dt>Kindle</dt>
> <dd>The Kindle is the revolutionary eReader from Amazon.com </dd>
> </dl>

<ol> </ol> Creates a numbered list
1. from enclosed
2. <li> tag items.</li>

<li> </li> Identifies an item in an number ordered or bullet unordered list.
<ul> </ul> Creates a bullet list
- from enclosed
- <li> tag items.</li>

Image Tag Demo

<img> is a placeholder for an image. This is an open tag, i.e. not paired. It must include the attribute-value pair src="URI". e.g. <img src="Kindle.jpg">. For Kindle Editions, this image must be include in compressed .zip file that is uploaded to DTP.

Links Tags Demo

<a> </a> Anchor for hyperlink.
A link to another page requires the attribute-value pair href="URL",
e.g. <a pair href="http://www.amazon.com">Amazon.com</a>.
An intra page link (also called a page "fragment") requires the attribute-value pair href="#FRAGMENT" ,
e.g. <a href="#ch1">Heading Tags Demo</a>.
The fragment must be tagged with either an anchor plus the attribute-value pair name="FRAGMENT" or with the attribute-value pair id="FRAGMENT" inside any other tag, e.g.
<a name="ch1">Chapter 1</a> or <h3 name="ch1">Chapter 1</h3>.
Fragment values must be unique, e.g. having two fragments identified as "ch1" will leave the links so named inoperable.

Bold Tag Demo

<b> </b> Formats enclosed text as <b>**bold**</b>.

Italic Tag Demo

<i> </i> Formats enclosed text as <i>*italic*</i>.

Font Tag Demos

<font> </font> Determines the appearance of the enclosed text.
It accepts the attribute-value pair size="N" (N may be a

number or number %),
Examples: <font size="1">size="1"</font> <font
size="2">size="2"</font> <font size="3">size="3"</font>
<font size="4">size="4"</font>

<font size="5">size="5"</font>

<font size="6">size="6"</font>

<font size="7">size="7"</font>

Other Text Tags Demos

<small> </small> Text is one point <small>smaller</small>
than the current size.
<s> </s> Formats text as <s> ~~strike through~~</s>.
<sub> </sub> Text as subscript, i.e. a reduced font size
and dropped below the baseline of the text<sub>$_a$</sub>.
<sup> </sup> Text as superscript, i.e. a reduced font size
and placed above the baseline, as in a reference to a
footnote<sup>[1] </sup>

Text Styles Demo

The text in Kindle Editions is not usually styled beyond
the basic type except for bold and italic words. Below are
a few examples to expand your page styling repertoire.

IN THE BEGINNING was a word, a reaction to

Kindle—the word, Y**ES**!

Here's the code for the above :
<font size="6">I</font><small>N THE BEGINNING</small> was a word, a reaction to Kindle—the word, <font size="4">Y</font><font size="5">E</font><font size="6">S!</font>

Drop caps can not be achieved in the Kindle. However, you can decorate with a text raised cap or image raised cap.

ccording to the authorities,
unnoticed; as, to turn work in
refreshes the tired person, m;

Stamp collectors may fairly c
it certainly makes time pass most agreeal
recreation, it is of such an engrossing chan
many tired mental workers need nowaday

Drop Cap Example

The beginning of a sentence can be decorated with a raised capital text character.
Text Raised Cap Example

he beginning of a sentence can be decorated with an raised capital image.
Image Raised Cap Example

Images in Books

DTP accepts images in the following formats for content in the book:
- Graphics Interchange Format (.gif)
- Portable Network Graphics (.png)
- Bitmap (.bmp)
- JPEG (.jpg)

NOTE that cover images <u>can only be</u> JPEG (.jpg) or TIFF(.tff).

Image tag example: <img src="some-name.jpg">.
The "align" attribute can be used, for example, <img src="some-name.jpg" align="top">

See Amazon DTP >> Support Home >> Formatting Guide >> Advanced HTML Formatting >> Document 28
DTP gives the following specifics.

1. Images larger than 450 by 550 pixels are always re-sized by DTP.
2. Images inside content need to be 64kb or smaller.
3. Keep the image in an aspect ration of 9 to 11, which causes it to be re-sized to take up as much screen space as possible.

Two good image creation and editing tools are Picasa and GIMP.

Here are some other guidelines for images inside content:

1. For full page images, res-size to 450px X 550px.
2. Convert color images to grayscale.
3. Convert images that have text or line art to .png.
4. Increase sharpness.

Cover Images

Cover images <u>can only be</u> JPEG (.jpg) or TIFF(.tff). Recommended size is 450px wide x 550px high (aspect ration of 9 to 11).

For eBooks that are created for sale, covers are a very important marketing tool. Books can be published in the Kindle Store without covers. Publishing without a cover image, however, is a missed opportunity to present a positive image to prospective buyers.

If you do not have an image editor, try Picasa and take a time to explore its features. Practice with a few images to get comfortable with all the image editing tools that it has. In the end, I think you will find it easy to learn, and satisfying when you have created an eye-catching cover.

Here are some examples of good (in my opinion) book covers at the Kindle Store:
This Year You Write Your Novel by Walter Mosley (Kindle Edition - Jan 8, 2009) Comment: This cover is a simple bright orange background with an inset yellow medium-width border line framing the text. The text is a serif font that is well sized and centered. This uncluttered design should immediately attract a browsing eye due to its color, and focus attention on the title and then the author.
(amazon.com/This-Year-Write-Your-Novel/dp/ B000S1LVLI)

Never Give Up! by Joyce Meyer (Kindle Edition - April 9, 2009) Comment: This cover uses a large sans-serif type face for the title. It uses different text and background

colors and has an off-center placement of the photo of the author.
(amazon.com/Never-Give-Up/dp/B001E0V108)

Against Medical Advice by James Patterson and Hal Friedman (Kindle Edition - Oct 20, 2008) Comment: This cover places top billing of the author's name, extra-large red title, and a full background image.
(amazon.com/Against-Medical-Advice/dp/B001ANYDPO)

Below are the covers created for the three example books covered in Chapter 4 "Book Design—Three Examples": fiction—*One Man in His Time*, nonfiction—*Americas Historical Documents*, and poetry—*Poems of Lowell, Millay, & Speyer*.

Book Cover for *One Man in His Time*

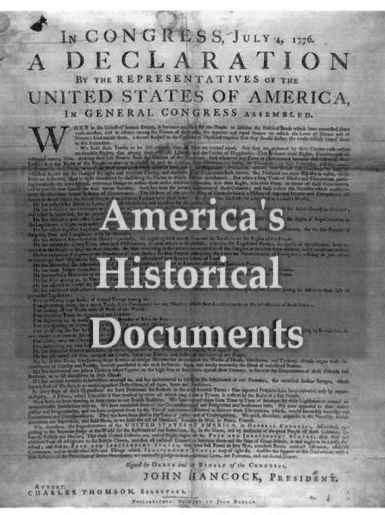

Book Cover for *America's Historical Documents*

Book Cover for *Poems of Lowell, Millay, & Speyer*

Next, we'll build three eBooks: one novel, one compilation of historical documents, and one anthology of poetry.

4
Book Design
Three Examples

Fiction Books | Nonfiction Books | Poetry Books

THIS CHAPTER will show how three Kindle Editions were built for publishing in the Kindle Store. For each book there are details about techniques and tools used, and time taken for each phase of the project.

Fiction Books

To demonstrate building a Kindle Edition from a work of fiction, I planned to use a novel that was in the public domain. After checking to be sure I had the right to copy and distribute the work from the source site, I saved the .html page to my computer. Here is a basic book plan that I drafted at the start of the project.

Book Plan

Book Genre
Kindle Book > Fiction

Readership
General Public

Text Length
300-600 KB

Tools
Firefox browser
Notepad text editor
Picasa image editor

Project Time
Editing source text into tag skeleton....15 minutes
Creating cover image..........................15 minutes
Publishing in DTP.............................15 minutes

Below is the template for HTML Tag Skeleton for Fiction Books used for this project.

Note that Kindle Editions don't need head sections. But you may find it helpful to include it. The title will show in the top title bar of your editor and browser. If you have several documents open in them, its easy to switch between documents when you can see their titles.

```
<html>
<head>
<title>TITLE</title>
</head>

<body>
<!--
REPLACE CAPITALIZED WORDS WITH YOUR INFO.
```

General Notes:

```
MY NOTES ABOUT THE BOOK,
TO-DO LIST
ETC.
-->
<!-- Below is the title page -->
<h1 align="left">TITLE </h1>

<h3 align="left">AUTHOR</h3>

Copyright © YEAR (e.g. 2008) AUTHOR

<mbp:pagebreak />
<br><br>
<!--
Text Body Notes:
MY NOTES ABOUT THIS SECTTION OF THE BOOK

-->
TEXT BODY
</body>
</html>
```

Below is an excerpt of the book's beginning and end content edited into the template. The editing consisted of:
1. searching in the copied file for "<h1>ONE MAN IN HIS TIME</h1>",
2. searching in the copied file for "<h1>END</h1>",
3. copying the content between those search terms and pasting it into the tag skeleton,
4. cutting the title page content and pasting it into the title page section of the skeleton.

```
<html>
<body>
<h1>ONE MAN IN HIS TIME</h1>

<h4>by</h4>

<h2>ELLEN GLASGOW</h2>

<h3>"One man in his time plays many parts."</h3>

NOTE<br>
No character in this book was drawn from any actual
person past or present.

<mbp:pagebreak />

<hr style="width: 65%;" />
<h2>CHAPTER I</h2>

<h3>THE SHADOW</h3>

<p>The winter's twilight, as thick as blown smoke, was
drifting through the Capitol Square. Already the snow
covered walks and the frozen fountains were in shadow;
but beyond the irregular black boughs of the trees the
sky was still suffused with the burning light of the
sunset. Over the head of the great bronze Washington a
single last gleam of sunshine shot suddenly before it
vanished amid the spires and chimneys of the city, which
looked as visionary and insubstantial as the glowing
horizon.</p>

...
```

<p>Passing the group in the hall, she went out on the porch, and looked with swimming eyes over the fountain into the Square. Beyond the white streams of electricity and the black patterns of the shadows, she saw the sharp outlines of the city, and beyond that the immense blue field of the sky sown thickly with stars. Life was there—life that embraced success and failure, illusion and disillusion, birth and death. In the morning she would go back to it—she would begin again—in the morning she would will herself to pick up the threads of middle age as lightly as Stephen and Patty would pick up the threads of youth. To-morrow she would start living again—but to-night for a few hours she would rest from life; she would look back now, as she had looked back that morning, to where a man was standing in the bright grass with the sunrise above his head.</p>
END
</body>
</html>

Visit Amazon's Kindle Store for *One Man in His Time* by Ellen Glasgow File Size: 347 KB, 199 pages

Nonfiction Books

This project demonstrates the inclusion of front matter sections and many chapters separated by page breaks. The book also demonstrates how to include images.

Tools
Firefox browser
Notepad text editor
Picasa image editor

Project Time
Creation of Title page, Dedication, Acknowledgement, and Introduction.... 2 hours
Adding Contents page entries.............. 5 minutes/entry
Editing source text into tag skeleton....10 minutes/entry (document)
Creating cover image.........................15 minutes
Publishing in DTP..............................15 minutes

Below is the template for HTML Tag Skeleton for Nonfiction Books used for this project.

```
<html>
<head>
<title>TITLE</title>
</head>

<body>
<!--
REPLACE CAPITALIZED WORDS WITH YOUR INFO.
```

General Notes:
MY NOTES ABOUT THE BOOK,
TO-DO LIST
ETC.
-->
<h1 align="left">TITLE</h1>

<h2 align="left">SUBTITLE</h2>

<h3 align="left">AUTHOR</h3>

Copyright © YEAR (e.g. 2008) AUTHOR

<mbp:pagebreak />
<!--
Section Notes:
MY NOTES ABOUT THIS SECTTION OF THE BOOK

-->
<h3 align="left">FRONT MATTER SECTION</h3>

TEXT

<mbp:pagebreak />
<!--
Section Notes:
MY NOTES ABOUT THIS SECTTION OF THE BOOK
-->
<h3 align="left">Contents</h3>

<a href="#ch1">CHAPTER TITLE</a>

<a href="#bck-sctn1">BACK MATTER SECTION</a>

```
<mbp:pagebreak />
<!--
Section Notes:
MY NOTES ABOUT THIS SECTTION OF THE BOOK
-->
<h3 align="left" id="ch1">CHAPTER TITLE</h3>

TEXT

<mbp:pagebreak />
<!--
Section Notes:
MY NOTES ABOUT THIS SECTTION OF THE BOOK
-->
<h3 align="left" id="bck-sctn1">BACK MATTER
SECTION</h3>

TEXT

</body>
</html>
```

Below is an excerpt of the book showing the front matter, and beginning and end sections of the body content. The source material was available in .html files. The editing consisted of:
1. generating original content for the front matter,
2. creating links for Contents,
3. copying the source content for each section' document after searching in the original for the beginning and end of the document text in the .html file, 4. adding images. Then, the text was pasted into the skeleton with an anchored heading (h4 align="left" id="UNIQUE-ID") to

the book body. This process was repeated for each document. The time for the project was obviously longer than the fiction example. Time was required to generate the front matter, to build the Contents page, and to add each document section and include images.

```
<html>
<body>
<h1 align="left">AMERICA'S HISTORICAL
DOCUMENTS</h1>

<h2 align="left">A Selection of Key Documents Dealing
with the<br />
Foundation, Growth, and Preservation of the<br />
United States of America</h2>

<h3 align="left">Preserved in the U.S. National
Archives</h3>

<h4>J. M. LaRoche, Editor</h4>

<mbp:pagebreak />

<h1><!--spacer--> </h1>

<h3 align="center">To<br>Dana</h3>

<h4 align="center">"The pen is mightier than the
sword."<br />
—Edward Bulwer-Lytton</h4>

<mbp:pagebreak />
```

<h1 align="left">ACKNOWLEDGEMENT</h1>

<h1><!--spacer--> </h1>

<h3 align="left">Images and transcriptions are from the National Archives and Records Administration</h3>

<mbp:pagebreak />

<h1 align="left">CONTENTS</h1>

<a href="#INTRODUCTION">INTRODUCTION</a>

<a href="#doc1">LEE RESOLUTION (1776)</a>
"Richard Henry Lee on June 7, 1776, introduced a resolution in the Second Continental Congress proposing independence for the colonies."

<a href="#doc2">THE DECLARATION OF INDEPENDENCE (1776)</a>
"Although the section of the Lee Resolution dealing with independence was not adopted until July 2, Congress appointed on June 10 a committee of five to draft a statement of independence for the colonies."

...

<a href="#doc42">TONKIN GULF RESOLUTION (1964)</a>
 "This joint resolution of Congress (H.J. RES 1145) dated August 7, 1964, gave President Lyndon Johnson authority to increase U.S. involvement in the war between North and South Vietnam."

Quotations from U.S. National Archives & Records

Administration.

<mbp:pagebreak />

<h1 align="left"
id="INTRODUCTION">INTRODUCTION</h1>

This is a collection of transcriptions of physical
documents housed in the U.S. National Archives,
Washington D.C. These documents attest to the
foundation, growth and preservation of our democracy.
They span almost two-hundred years of the history of
our country from its conception through to
mid-twentieth-century. The selection of documents is a
sampling of important agreements, legislation,
resolutions, speeches, and treaties, some prosaic in
wording, others written with great eloquence. All of
them are important to what our nation now is.

For one-hundred-fifty years, the original documents were
not housed in a dedicated archive. Important
government documents were lost due to fires and
neglect. In 1926, Congress approved the establishment of
the National Archives Building. In the last months of
1935, staff members began moving into an uncompleted
building. In the late 1960s, the building's storage capacity
of 900,000 cubic feet was full. In 1993, a second National
Archives building was completed in College Park,
Maryland. When built, its 1.8 million square was the
most modern archives facility in the world.

<img src="img-pbk/US_National_Archives.jpg">
U.S. National Archives, Washington D.C.

"The development of the U.S. archival profession and timeline for the National Archives:
1800 Fires damaged records of the War Office and the Treasury Department from 1800-1801
1861-1865 Number of federal records surged and the Government grew during Civil War...

<mbp:pagebreak />

<h1 align="left" id="doc1">LEE RESOLUTION (1776)</h1>

<p>Resolved, That these United Colonies are, and of right ought to be, free and independent States, that they are absolved from all allegiance to the British Crown, and that all political connection between them and the State of Great Britain is, and ought to be, totally dissolved.</p>
<p>That it is expedient forthwith to take the most effectual measures for forming foreign Alliances. </p>

<p>That a plan of confederation be prepared and transmitted to the respective Colonies for their consideration and approbation.</p>

<mbp:pagebreak />

<h1 align="left" id="doc2">THE DECLARATION OF INDEPENDENCE (1776)</h1>

<p class="heading">IN CONGRESS, July 4, 1776.</p>

<p><b>The unanimous Declaration of the thirteen united States of America,</b></p>

<p>When in the Course of human events, it becomes necessary for one people to dissolve the political bands which have connected them with another, and to assume among the powers of the earth, the separate and equal station to which the Laws of Nature and of Nature's God entitle them, a decent respect to the opinions of mankind requires that they should declare the causes which impel them to the separation.</p> <p>We hold these truths to be self-evident, that all men are created equal, that they are endowed by their Creator with certain unalienable Rights, that among these are Life, Liberty and the pursuit of Happiness.—That to secure these rights, Governments are instituted among Men, deriving their just powers from the consent of the governed, —That whenever any Form of Government becomes destructive of these ends, it is the Right of the People to alter or to abolish it, and to institute new Government, laying its foundation on such principles and organizing its powers in such form, as to them shall seem most likely to effect their Safety and Happiness. Prudence, indeed, will dictate that Governments long established should not be changed for light and transient causes; and accordingly all experience hath shewn, that mankind are more disposed to suffer, while evils are sufferable, than to right themselves by abolishing the forms to which they are accustomed. But when a long train of abuses and usurpations, pursuing invariably the same Object evinces a design to reduce them under absolute Despotism, it is their right, it is their duty, to throw off such Government, and to provide new Guards for their future security.—Such has been the patient sufferance of these Colonies; and such is now the necessity which constrains them to alter their former Systems of Government. The history of the present King

of Great Britain is a history of repeated injuries and usurpations, all having in direct object the establishment of an absolute Tyranny over these States. To prove this, let Facts be submitted to a candid world.</p>

<p>He has refused his Assent to Laws, the most wholesome and necessary for the public good.
...
<mbp:pagebreak />

<h1 align="left" id="doc42">TONKIN GULF RESOLUTION (1964)</h1>

<p><b>Eighty-eighth Congress of the United States of America</b>
AT THE SECOND SESSION</p>
<p><i>Begun and held at the City of Washington on Tuesday, the seventh day of January, one thousand nine hundred and sixty-four</i></p>
<p>Joint Resolution
To promote the maintenance of international peace and security in southeast Asia....

</body>
</html>

Visit Amazon's Kindle Store for *America's Historical Documents* J.M. LaRoche, Editor, File Size: 316 KB, 221 pages.

Next we'll cover the design of a book of poetry.

Poetry Books

Tools
Firefox browser
Notepad text editor
Picasa image editor

Project Time
Creation of Title page and About the Authors.... 2 hours
Adding Contents page entries.............. 5 minutes/entry
Editing source text into tag skeleton....10 minutes/entry
(poem)
Creating cover image........................15 minutes
Publishing in DTP.............................15 minutes

This poetry anthology is a variation of the previous
nonfiction project in tag structure. The front matter
consists of a title page and contents page. Building this
book was time consuming due to the number of poems.
The process was straightforward in repetition of adding a
title link in the contents page for a poem, then adding
that poem with an anchored heading (h4 align="left"
id="UNIQUE-ID") to the book body. Those two steps
were repeated for each poem. This book has each poem
separated by a page break. That is a style choice of book
design. It could just as well be designed without any
page breaks in the book body like the fiction book
example.

Unlike prose paragraphs, poetry requires formatting
with many line breaks. If the original content is available
as an .html file it is probably "ready to go." If you see
that an .html source has poems contained within <pre>

</pre> tags, those tags must be deleted and breaks added after each poem line. Kindle does not support the preformat tag. Those with PERL programming experience can use a module to make short work of the chore of adding end-of-line break tags and then run a script to do it in one fell swoop.

As the book excerpt below shows, these poems all have their lines flush with the left margin. Often lines of poetry will have alternate indented lines. This can be accomplished by inserting one or more " " no-break-spaces at the beginning of a line to force indentation.

Some other types of content may be presented with line breaks in lieu of bullet lists or numbered lists, e.g. ingredients in cookbooks, parts lists for constructing objects, and organization members lists.

```
<html>
<body>
<h1 align="left">Poems of Lowell, Millay, & Speyer</h1>

<h2 align="left">Collected Poems of Three Women Poets
<br>
Who Won the Pulitzer</h2>

<br><br>

<h3 align="left">J.M. LaRoche, Editor</h3>

<mbp:pagebreak />
```

\<h2 align="left">Contents\</h2>

\<h3 align="left">\<a href="#About">About the
Authors\</a>\</h3>

\<h3 align="left">Poems by Amy Lowell\</h3>

\\<font size="+1">A Dome of Many-coloured
Glass\</font>\
Lyrical Poems\\
\<a href="#AL1">Before the Altar\</a>\

\<mbp:pagebreak />

\<h3 align="left">Poems by Edna St. Vincent Millay\</h3>

\A Few Figs from Thistles, Poems and
Sonnets\\
\<a href="#EM1">First Fig\</a>\
...

\<mbp:pagebreak />

\<h3 align="left">Poems of Leonora Speyer\</h3>

\<a href="#LS1">April On The Battlefields\</a>\

\<mbp:pagebreak />

\<h3 id="About">About the Authors\</h3>

\Amy Lawrence Lowell\ (1874-1925) was an
American poet...

```
<mbp:pagebreak />

<h3 id="AL1">Poems by Amy Lowell<br /><br />
A Dome of Many-coloured Glass</h3>


"Life, like a dome of many-coloured glass,<BR>
Stains the white radiance of Eternity."<BR>
—Shelley, "Adonais".
<BR><BR>

<i>"Le silence est si grand que mon coeur en
frissonne,<BR>
Seul, le bruit de mes pas sur le pave resonne."</i><BR>
—Albert Samain.<br />

<h4 align="left" id="AL1">Before the Altar</h4>

Before the Altar, bowed, he stands<br>
With empty hands;<br>
Upon it perfumed offerings burn<br>
Wreathing with smoke the sacrificial urn.<br>
Not one of all these has he given,<br>
No flame of his has leapt to Heaven<br>
Firesouled, vermilion-hearted,<br>
Forked, and darted,<br>
Consuming what a few spare pence<br>
Have cheaply bought, to fling from hence<br>
In idly-asked petition.<br>
...

<mbp:pagebreak />

<h4 align="left" id="LS8">Sekhmet the Lion-Headed</h4>
```

In the dark night I heard a stirring,
Near me something was purring.

A voice, deep-throated, spoke:

I litter armies for all easts and wests
And norths and souths:
They suckle my girl-goddess breasts,
And my fierce milk drips from their mouths.

The voice sang:

...
</body>
</html>

Visit Amazon's Kindle Store for *Poems of Lowell, Millay, & Speyer* J.M. LaRoche, Editor, File Size: 91 KB.

Next, I'll show how to publish your book for sale in Amazon's Kindle Store.

5
Publish a Kindle Edition

AMAZON'S DIGITAL TEXT PLATFORM (DTP) is the online publishing tool at http://dtp.amazon.com that enables you to publish your book for sale in the Kindle Store. If you have an Amazon account, you can sign in at the front page. If you don't have an account, there is a button to click to sign up for one. The front page also has links to FAQs and Community Forums.

The DTP interface is straight forward and user-friendly. We'll review the entry steps in the form and offer some caveats about possible problems. But, before we do let's look at step 5 of Checklist for Commercial Kindle Editions.

Checklist for Commercial Kindle Editions

Note: capitalized words are stand-ins for your names.

5. Publishing

Zip up My Documents/KEP/KEP TITLE-1/TITLE.html. If there are images, add images/ to TITLE.zip.
Create TITLE_cover.jpg.
Create a blurb and "Save As" TITLE_Blurb.txt (4,000

characters maximum).

Create TITLE_Keywords.txt , add a list of keywords appropriate to your book's content, the more the better, aim for a dozen.

Sign in at DTP, click "Add new item".

1. Enter Product Details:

fill in Title,

fill in Description copying Blurb.txt,

add Publisher and date,

select Categories,

fill in Authors,

fill in Search Keywords copying Keywords.txt,

upload Product Image (TITLE_cover.jpg),

Save entries.

2. Upload and Preview Book:

upload TITLE.zip & proofread the book in Preview Mode.

3. Enter Price:

fill in price and Save.

Click "Publish".

24 hours after publishing, visit the Kindle Store and check that your book is listed, proofread the title and author.

72 hours after publishing, visit the Kindle Store and proofread your description.

It is important that you have the first four items of step 5 completed before signing in to publish.

1. Enter Product Details. After you click "Add new", DTP presents a form to "Enter Product Details." The form fields only accept plain text. Do not enter HTML tags or non UTF-8 characters. If you plan to paste in text, be sure the the original document is UTF-8 encoded.

1. Enter Product Details

The first fill-in box is for an **ISBN**. Enter yours for your book if you have one. A key feature of DTP is that you can publish without an ISBN. Note that the there is a red asterisk after each item label that is required to have data filled in.

The next field to fill is **Title**. Note that this field by default is pre-filled with "New Title 1" When you start to type your title into the box, the default words will disappear. Be sure to type your title into the title box. You may think this is stating the obvious. However, I recently (9/14/08) searched the Kindle Store for Kindle Editions titled "New Title 1". The search returned 72! I also found other titles with errors caused by cut and paste of text with non UTF-8 encoding: "*The Gifted Gabald?n Sisters* by Lorraine L?pez (Kindle Edition - Oct 1, 2008)" (question mark displays in lieu of apostrophe), "*Manon Lescaut by Abb?, Pr?vost* (Kindle Edition - Sep 15,

2008)".(question mark displays in lieu of accented letters)

Here is an example of an error caused by entering HTML tags, "*Happiness For Dummies®* by W. Doyle, PhD Gentry (Kindle Edition - Oct 27, 2008)".

Here are examples of typos (1st & 2nd titles have incomplete words, 3rd title has a missing word), "*The Woun Heart* by Dan B. Allender (Kindle Edition - Sep 15, 2008)", "*Electing a US Pr in Plain English* by Lee & Sachi LeFever (Kindle Edition - Sep 10, 2008)", "*Sarah: How a Hockey Turned the Political Establishment Upside-Down* by Kaylene Johnson (Kindle Edition - Sep 10, 2008)".

The next field to fill is **Description**. Here is where your Blurb.txt can be pasted. Description accepts up to 4,000 characters (UTF-8 encoded). If you use Microsoft Word, find Word Count in the Tools menu. The blurb for this book has 2,240 characters with spaces:

Here is a *proven* step-by-step method for getting eBooks built and published for Amazon's Kindle eReader by an experienced publisher of Kindle Editions.

The author has helped content creators through editing, book layout, cover design, publication, and promotion for eBooks and print-on-demand books. Since the arrival of the Kindle, he has been involved daily in producing books according to the Amazon's requirements for Kindle Editions. He has organized *Build a Kindle Edition—Anyone Can!* as a guide and reference tool.

Here is a road map for building a personal eBook, or for making one to publish in the Kindle Store. Experienced and would-be authors will find clear explanations of proven techniques that enable them to create, publish, and promote an eBook in a short time. The author's approach is not hype and theory. He uses three book building projects that have been published to show how his methods work. The first book building project covers a work of fiction. The second deals with the requirements of a nonfiction book. The third shows the particular details of building an anthology of poetry.

If you ever thought about writing, but hesitated after realizing how hard it can be to have a book published through the old publishing establishment, here is a method to achieve your aspirations. Amazon's revolutionary Kindle eReader along with its Digital Text Platform for publishing has democratized the industry. Now, YOU can create and market your eBook. *Carpe diem*!

The book is a practical tutorial that explains, through building three example Kindle Editions, how to create books for personal use or for sale at the Kindle Store.
Contents:
1 Anyone Can Build a Kindle Edition: The New Paradigm of Open Publishing
2 Book Content: Text and Images
3 Book building: Techniques and Tools
4 Book Design—Three Examples: Fiction, Nonfiction, & Poetry
5 Publish a Kindle Edition: Amazon's Digital Text Platform
6 Promote Your Kindle Edition: Timeline of Marketing Activities
7 Recommended Reading: Kindle Editions about

Publishing & Writing
8 eBook Timeline: Milestones in the History of eBooks, and eBook Readers
9 Online Resources: Services & Tools
10 Kindle HTML Tags: The Complete List
11 Glossary

The next field to fill is **Publisher**. Note this is optional. I don't know why, but as with cover images, I have seen instances where there is no publisher on a book product page. In my opinion, leaving this blank is a missed opportunity to advertise.

The next field to fill is **Publication Date**. Note this is optional. If you do not enter a date, the publication date will show as the date which you clicked Publish. You can select a future date to advise prospective buyers. They then have the ability to pre-order and will receive the book at that future publication date. Setting a future publication date could give you time to submit review copies in HTML format and gather endorsements to quote on your product page.

The next field to fill is **Categories**. After you click the Add/Edit button, DTP presents a list of selectable categories. You can select a maximum of five categories for your book.
Here are the ones selected for this book:
Kindle Books > Nonfiction > General
Kindle Books > Business & Investing > General
Kindle Books > Computers & Internet > Hardware
Kindle Books > Reference Publishing & Books > Authorship
Kindle Books > Nonfiction > Reference > Writing

The next field to fill is **Authors**. This is required. If your book is a collaboration, you can add additional author names. There is a pull-down menu where you can select different titles: Author, Editor, Illustrator, Narrator, Photographer, Foreword, Introduction, Translator.

The next field to fill is **Keywords**. These help readers searching for books in the Kindle Store. Paste in yours from your Keywords.txt. Here are keywords for this book: do-it-yourself, how-to, step-by-step, guide, hands-on, projects, free examples, HTML tutorial, cover design, book building, bookbuilders, book layout, book design, authors, book promotion, book publicity, self-publishing, publishing guide, ebooks, kindle, electronic books, ereaders, electronic readers, digital readers

The next item is **Edition Number**. DTP enables you to update your book anytime. If you expect to have updated information, notices of corrections, or expanded content, enter "1st" (or "First") here. Note that DTP will add the word "edition" for you. If you enter "1st edition" or "First edition", DTP will display it on the product page as"1st edition edition" or "First edition edition".

The next item is **Series Title**. An example of when this field might be filled is the case of my associate, Tim, who is planning a series of books, "Tim's Travel Logs."

The next item is **Series Volume**. For example "Vol. I".

The next item is **Product Image**. Note that Amazon does not require a cover image. Personally, I can not think of one reason why a publisher would not include a cover image. Yet, there are many titles published without one. If your image is smaller than the minimum size or the wrong file type, DTP will refuse the upload and display the cause of error. When you have fixed the image click upload again. If at anytime in the future you want a different image, click upload and the new image will replace the old one.

When you have finished entering your Product Details, click Save entries. DTP will confirm "saved." at the side of the Save button,

Another key feature of DTP is that you can modify any entry item in the future. Note that after editing data of a published title, you must click Publish to affect the change.

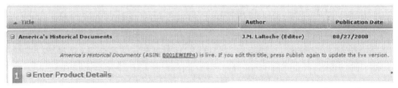

"If you edit this title, press Publish again to update the live version."

2. Upload & Preview Book
The next major step is to click Browse, select your compressed (.zip) file from your computer and click Upload. It should only take about half-a-minute to convert your file. If it is taking longer, refresh your browser and upload again.

"Your file is converting, please wait..."

When your file is converted a Preview button should appear to the right of the Upload button. From time to time I have experienced that the Preview button does not appear after the file has been converted. If this happens, got to step 3, enter your data and Save, then go back to step 2, the Preview button should now be visible.

Notice of successful document upload

If you get an error notice, the left panel has Advanced: Download & Modify HTML. Click the downward arrow to expose the Download button. Download your file and correct the problem. The most likely error is malformed HTML. Check your file with an HTML validator. Users of the Firefox Web Browser can get a free HTML validator. Web Developer add-on. When you use the validator, ignore warnings about <!DOCTYPE>and <mbp:pagebreak>.

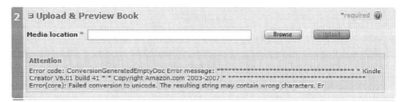

Notice of unsuccessful document upload—error in HTML

After clicking Preview there may be a few seconds delay before the first page of your book appears in the right side preview panel. If you receive notice that "This page is not available", refresh your browser.

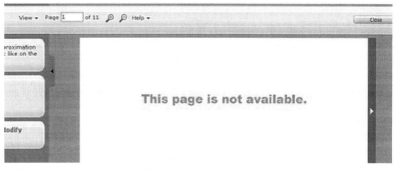

"This page is not available"

Now, take time and preview all your book pages. If you have images, they will be positioned correctly, but may be reduced in size. The full image size will display in the Kindle. For example, below are two covers from the example books. The size of each is 450px wide x 550px high. Each cover should take up the space of one page in the Kindle. The image below shows that Preview has reduced their size so there are two images on the preview page, both are correctly centered.

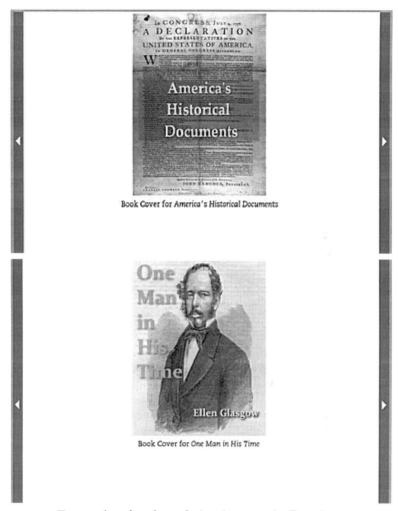

Book Cover for America's Historical Documents

Book Cover for One Man in His Time

Example of reduced size images in Preview

If you notice any typos or anything you want to change, click the downward arrow of the left side Download and Modify HTML box. The box will expand to expose the Download button. Download your file; correct the error(s) in the file, re-upload, and preview it again.

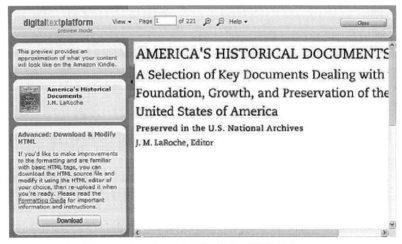

Preview's "Download and Modify HTML"

In the above image notice the top tool bar. It has several handy features. View offers a scrolling view option. Page shows the number of the page that you are previewing and the total number of book pages. If you want to jump to a particular page, type the page number in the white box. For instance, if you want to go to the end of a one-hundred page book, type 100 in the box and hit Enter on your keyboard. Because Preview shows images smaller than they will be in the Kindle, the Preview page may undercount the actual page count. The left pane maybe hidden by clicking the leftward pointing black arrow that is between the left and right panes. This gives a fuller view of the book pages to concentrate on when you proofread. You can navigate to the next page and to the previous page by clicking the white arrows at the sides of the page preview panel.

3. Enter Price
The price field accepts minimum price of $0.99 to a

maximum of $200.00. Enter you price and click Save.

Publish

Click the Publish button. DTP then shows that your content is being published. Note that after clicking Publish you cannot edit this title until it is live. Congratulations! Your Kindle Edition should appear in the Kindle Store catalog in 12 to 72 hours.

⬆ Title	Author
Publishing *America's Historical Documents*. Your content is being published. It will be live in 12 to 72 hours. (why?)	

"Your content is being published. It will be live in 12 to 72 hours."

Closing Comments

Maximize your Description and Keywords.
Proofread. Proofread. Proofread.

Visit Amazon Digital Platform Community Support Forums:
Amazon DTP >> Support Home >> Forums Home >> Ask the Community for advice.

Next, we'll plan a campaign to publicize your Kindle Edition.

6
Promote Your Kindle Edition

YOU HAVE done the grunt work in putting your book together and published it. Now for the fun part—chatting up your masterpiece! The following are some things to do to get your book in the limelight.

Timetable of Marketing Activities

12-72 Hours After Clicking the DTP "Publish" Button

Visit the Kindle Book Store to be certain that your book is there. Check the title, author, and publisher to make sure there are no typos. If there are errors, sign in to DTP, correct them, "Save" the new info and click "Publish" again. About 72 hours later Amazon will include the Description on the book's page. Proofread the description for accuracy.

After the Kindle Store book's page is complete email your book's HTML file to colleagues and friends. Let them know that you have published it as an Amazon Kindle Edition. Ask them to comment on the work. Add their endorsement quotes to your book's description.

Create alerts at Yahoo! (http://alerts.yahoo.com/) or Google (http://www.google.com/alerts) for "TITLE", "AUTHOR", & "PUBLISHER". You will be alerted of any mention of those words on the web. You might find that bloggers or other web sites are mentioning your work in either good light or bad. This can be an opportunity to gather additional endorsement quotes, or enable you to quickly reply to negative comments.

Become an Amazon Associate. "Associates is Amazon.com's affiliate marketing program." (https://affiliate-program.amazon.com/gp/associates/join/). When customers order products by clicking a link that has your ID, you'll receive a commission for the sale. Use your book's ASIN and build a link. Here's an example: <a href="http://www.amazon.com/dp/B001FOQT4G/ ?tag=YOUR-ID">One Man in His Time</a> by Ellen Glasgow. The URL is easy to decipher. The domain name amazon.com/ followed by the directory dp/ (abbreviation for digital product?) followed by the Amazon Stock Identification Number, followed by "/?tag=YOUR-ID".

Start a blog about your book. Advertise your book AND the Kindle eReader at your blog, and at any other Web sites that you may already have. The Amazon Associates site is very user friendly. It can provide many ways to present the products with Web page widgets that are coded with your ID.

Update your email signature with the book title and book page URL .

Update any online profiles that you have, e.g. Amazon

and LinkedIn, with info about your book.

Use your printer to make a batch of fliers. Create a .doc, .html, or .pdf file of your book description, cover image, and Amazon page URL. Print copies for hand-outs, or to place on bulletin boards, on your office desk, or reception area tables, etc.

Join Kindle Korner (http://groups.yahoo.com/group/kindlekorner). This is the largest forum of Kindle owners. They are a great group of people who are generous with their advice and general comments. Don't be shy. Let them know you are a new Kindle Edition publisher. End your forum posts with your name and the URL of your book's blog. Some may have purchased your book and offer their opinion about it.

72 Hours After Publishing

Send a press release to your local newspapers and radio/ TV. Also, do a Google search for "free press releases". The Online Resources section has links to several services that send out press releases for free.

Submit review copies. Does your newspaper have a book reviewer? Send the reviewer a copy of your flier and the book's HTML file with a cover letter.

Contact local public libraries, churches, schools, clubs, and civic service organizations. Let them know you are available as a speaker. Set up a "Meet the Author" night to talk about the book's subject and other areas of your expertise that can benefit their audiences.

Cultivate reporter contacts. Local media need expert sources. Join HelpAReporter.com
This is a free service that feeds queries to registered members from reporters who are looking for expert sources.

Stay active with reading and replying at the blogs that you visit, and forums that you are a member of. Mention your book when and where appropriate. A few that I like are
Amazon Kindle's Blog
http://www.amazon.com/gp/blog/A1F8Z0JAEIDVRY
The Kindle Reader
http://kindlereader.blogspot.com/
Kindleville
http://kindleville.blogspot.com/

Ask buyers of your Kindle Edition to rate it with some stars at Amazon.

Print calling cards. In addition to your name, phone, & email, include "Author of YOUR BOOK TITLE Kindle Edition", Amazon product URL e.g. www.amazon.com/dp/YOUR-ASIN/, and your blog URL.

Use your Kindle in public places. When approached about the device give a quick demo and talk about its features:
1. paper-like display provides comfortable reading—no eye fatigue as from the glare of computer displays,
2. long time between battery charges,
3. 200 books storage,
4. reasonable book costs,

5. Kindle Store has more than 175,000 books, and growing daily,
6. Kindle Store has magazines, newspapers, & blogs,
7. plays Audio Books and other MP3 files,
8. Whispernet web connectivity,
9. Internet browser,
10. keyboard for text input,
11. document conversion service,
12. anyone can publish, just like YOU did.

Now, don't forget to tell them about *your Kindle Edition* and offer one of your cards with your book's information.

We are at the end of this book's tutorial content. The following sections list resources to help you in your book projects.

I wish you every success in publishing your Kindle Edition. You can do it!

eBook sales were $33 million in 2007

7
Recommended Reading

OME informative Kindle Editions follow:

Graphics on the Kindle by Manuel Burgos
"Learn how to edit photos and apply special effects written specifically for the Kindle to make your images look significantly better in your e-book.—Amazon You'll also learn how to use clip-art and graphical text elements to add extra visual power to your e-books."

Benjamin Franklin by Walter Isaacson
"Following closely on the heels of Edmund Morgan's justly acclaimed Benjamin Franklin, Isaacson's longer biography easily holds its own. How do the two books differ? Isaacson's is more detailed; it lingers over such matters as the nature of Franklin's complex family circumstances and his relations with others, and it pays closer attention to each of his extraordinary achievements."—Publishers Weekly

Copyright Plain & Simple by Cheryl Besenjak
"The fundamental elements of copyright protection are explained in a simple, effective volume important to any writer. The basics of copyright law is explained through numerous clear examples and discussions of the foundations of protection; from applications to music

and electronics to fair use policies." —Midwest Book Review

On Writing by Stephen King
"Short and snappy as it is, Stephen King's On Writing really contains two books: a fondly sardonic autobiography and a tough-love lesson for aspiring novelists." —Amazon

The Book on Writing: The Ultimate Guide to Writing Well by Paula LaRocque
"The Book on Writing contains 25 chapters in three sections: 1) A dozen essential guidelines to good writing, from the importance of short sentences to the value of using a conversational tone; 2) How to tell a story - how to build suspense, how to effectively describe things, how to use literary devices; and 3) A concise handbook on writing mechanics, such as grammar, usage, punctuation, and style." —Amazon

8
eBook Timeline

M ILESTONES in the History of eBooks, & eBook Readers:

1971 Michael Hart publishes first eBook, a copy of the Declaration of Independence. Hart later establishes Project Gutenberg.
1981 Random House publishes dictionary as electronic book.
1991 Tim Berners-Lee invents HTML.
1991 E-print servers begin—now arXiv.org "arXiv is an e-print service in the fields of physics, mathematics, non-linear science, computer science, quantitative biology and statistics... owned, operated and funded by Cornell University..."—arxiv.org
1991 Project Gutenberg begins digitizing one book per month.
1992 University of North Carolina developed SunSITE which became ibiblio.
1993 The Portable Document Format (PDF) is created by Adobe.
1995 HighWire Press, a division of the Stanford University Libraries "hosts the largest repository of free full-text life science articles in the world"—highwire.stanford.edu/about/
1996 The Internet Archive was founded by Brewster

Kahle.

1998 Rocket Ebook handheld LCD eBook reading device.

1998 First International Electronic Book Workshop held by U.S. National Institute of Standards and Technology (NIST). **1999** Ebrary.com established.

1999 The Franklin eBookMan handheld LCD eBook reading device.

2000 Microsoft Reader using ClearType subpixel rendering technology for displaying eBooks in .lit format, was available as a free Windows program.

2000 "Mobipocket Reader, a universal reader for PDAs. Mobipocket.com was bought by Amazon.com in 2005."—wikipedia.org/wiki/Mobipocket

2000 Public Library of Science (PLoS) was established.—plos.org/about/index.html

2001 *Riding the Bullet* by Stephen King was launched exclusively on the Web.

2001 Gemstar REB 100 handheld LCD eBook reading device.

2001 O'Reilly Media, Inc. and The Pearson Technology Group create Safari Books Online.—safaribooksonline.com/company/company.php

2002 OverDrive launched Digital Library Reserve extending eBook services to libraries.—overdrive.com/aboutus/

2004 Librié by Sony.—first eReader to use E Ink available in Japan.

2004 Google Books is launched.

2006 Sony Reader PRS 500 is made available in U.S.

2006 iRex iLiad handheld eReader with 9" E Ink display is manufactured in Europe.

2007 Sony Reader markets PRS 505 with 2nd generation E Ink Vizplex display.

2007 The Boston Library Consortium, Inc. (BLC) partners

with the Open Content Alliance (OCA).

2007 Amazon.com markets the Kindle eReader with E Ink display, Whispernet content delivery, and the Digital Text Platform (DTP).

2007 eBook sales were up 59% in 2007 as compared to sales in 2006 according to *Business Week*.

2007 eBook sales were $33 million in 2007, a rise from $6 million in 2002 (2007 publishing industry total sales were $25 billion) according to IDPF.org.

2008 Author George Soros has *The New Paradigm for Financial Markets: The Credit Crisis of 2008 and What It Means* published in eBook format prior to print publication.

9
Online Resources

Aids for Writing | Editing Software
Public Domain Content | Promotion

Aids for Writing

The Chicago Manual of Style Online
(chicagomanualofstyle.org)
"the indispensable online reference for all who work
with words."
Dictionary.com
Online Dictionary and Thesaurus "...a multi-source
dictionary search service..."
OWL (http://owl.english.purdue.edu/)
"The Purdue Online Writing Lab"
U.S. Copyright Office (copyright.gov)
"Copyright Basics, Copyright Law, Current Fees," etc.

Editing Software

Dragon NaturallySpeaking (Amazon.com/
Dragon_NaturallySpeaking)
"Dictate and edit in virtually any Windows application",
e.g. Internet Explorer, Mozilla Firefox.
GNU Image Manipulation Program—GIMP for
Windows (gimp-win.sourceforge.net)

GIMP is a free image creator/editor for Windows 2000/XP/Vista.

Google's Picasa (picasa.com)

Picasa is a free image editor for Windows XP/Vista.

Ron Burkey's GutenMark (sandroid.org/GutenMark/)

GutenMark is a free tool for "automatically creating high-quality HTML or LaTeX markup from Project Gutenberg etexts ... Both Windows and Linux 'x86 are supported. Mac OS X is also supported, though in some respects it lags the others. Limited iPhone support is also possible."

Text editor Notepad++ (notepad-plus.sourceforge.net)

"Notepad++ is a free ... source code editor and Notepad replacement that supports several languages. It runs in the MS Windows environment.."

OpenOffice (openoffice.org) is a free alternative to Microsoft Office. It's Writer wordprocessor is a great tool for converting .doc files to .html files.

Scintilla.org's SciTE (scintilla.org)

A great text editor for both novice and veteran programmers.

Virdi Software's Text2Web Pro (virdi-software.com)

"Text2Web Pro is a free tool to convert text documents to html format" for Windows 95/98/Me/NT/2000/XP.

Public Domain Content

Bartleby.com
"Since its incorporation in 1999 and the release of preeminent contemporary reference works, Bartleby.com becomes the most comprehensive reference publisher on the web, meeting the needs of students, educators, and the intellectually curious."
Bibliomania.com
"Free Online Literature with more than 2000 Classic Texts"
The Brown University Women Writers Project (www.wwp.brown.edu)
"The Brown University Women Writers Project is a long-term research project devoted to early modern women's writing and electronic text encoding."
Digital Book Index (digitalbookindex.com)
"Digital Book Index provides links to more than 141,000 full-text digital books."
University of Virginia Library's Etext Center (etext.virginia.edu/ebooks)
"Over 2,100 publicly-available ebooks from the University of Virginia Library's Etext Center, including classic British and American fiction, major authors, children's literature, American history, Shakespeare, African-American documents, the Bible, and much more."
Emory Women Writers Resource Project (chaucer.library.emory.edu/wwrp)
"The Emory Women Writers Resource Project is a collection of edited and unedited texts by women writing in English from the seventeenth century through the nineteenth century."

ibiblio (ibiblio.org)
"The public's library and digital archive."
The Internet Public Library (ipl.org)
"The Internet Public Library is a public service
organization and a learning/teaching environment
founded at the University of Michigan School of
Information and hosted by Drexel University's College of
Information Science & Technology."
Library of Congress Digital Collections & Services
(loc.gov)
Online access to print, pictorial and audio-visual
collections and other digital services
National Archives and Records Administration
(archives.gov)
Many exhibits at the site display public domain
documents and images. Visit Today's Document from the
National Archives (archives.gov/historical-docs/
todays-doc) and Online Exhibits (archives.gov/exhibits)
The Online Books Page (onlinebooks.library.upenn.edu)
Hosted by the University of Pennsylvania Libraries,
"Listing over 30,000 free books on the Web."
Project Gutenberg (gutenberg.org)
"There are over 25,000 free books in the Project
Gutenberg Online Book Catalog."
WikiMedia (wikimedia.org)
Commons:Reusing content outside Wikimedia

Publishing Services

HTMPulishing (htmpublishing.net)
Book design, cover design, and editing for eBooks and print-on-demand paperbacks.

Promotion

Blogs & Blogging
Amazon Kindle's Blog (amazon.com/gp/blog/A1F8Z0JAEIDVRY)
The Kindle Reader (kindlereader.blogspot.com)
Kindleville (kindleville.blogspot.com)
Blogger (blogger.com)
Free blog publishing and hosting.

Forums:
Amazon Kindle Forum
Amazon's Forum
Customer Discussions: Kindle: Amazon's New Wireless Reading Device forum
Yahoo! Groups:
Kindle Korner (groups.yahoo.com/group/kindlekorner/)
The most highly trafficed forum about the Kindle.
All Nonfiction (groups.yahoo.com/group/All_Nonfiction/)
allaboutmurder (groups.yahoo.com/group/allaboutmurder/)
BookCrazy (groups.yahoo.com/group/BookCrazy/)
books (groups.yahoo.com/group/books/)
booksamonth (groups.yahoo.com/group/booksamonth/)
MarketingTravelBooks (groups.yahoo.com/group/MarketingTravelBooks/)

paranormalromance (groups.yahoo.com/group/
paranormalromance/)
RomanceJunkiesReaders (groups.yahoo.com/group/
RomanceJunkiesReaders/)
ScienceFantasyFictio (groups.yahoo.com/group/
ScienceFantasyFictio/)

Social Networking
Facebook.com
One of the most highly trafficked social network sites.
LinkedIn.com
A high visibility networking site.

Media
HelpAReporter.com
Free service that feeds queries from reporters looking for
expert sources.
1888PressRelease.com
"Services include free press release submission, press
release distribution."
24-7PressRelease.com
"Submitting press releases with 24-7 Press Release is
always FREE."
PR9.net
"You can submit your the press releases to this site for
free."
PressReleaseRoom.com
"This site only accepts unique news releases that have
not been posted elsewhere on the Web. "
PRLog.org
"PRLog is a free online press release service. "
PRZOOM.com
"PRZOOM is a free press releases & news distribution
service to corporations, PR agencies, market research,

business journalists, freelance writers, news content providers."

10
Kindle HTML Tags

Document Structure | Images | Links
Lists | Text | Page Elements
Alphabetical Tag List

HTML documents consist of:
document structure elements,
page block-level elements—such as headings,
paragraphs, divisions, and lists, which can include
images and text.
Tags—paired, or open, can include attribute-value pairs.
Tags are case insensitive, e.g.
 or <br> is OK. Open
tags can be with or without an end dash, e.g.
.
Tags must be *nested correctly*. Examples: incorrect
nesting: nested incorrectly, correct nesting:
nested correctly
Special Character Entities code numbers can be included.

For a complete HTML tutorial visit W3Schools.com.

For advice from experienced Kindle Edition publishers
visit Amazon Digital Platform's Community Support
Forums.

Document Structure
<html></html> All Kindle HTML files must include these.
<body></body> All Kindle HTML files must include
these.

Page Elements

<mbp:pagebreak /> starts a new page in Kindle. This is not an official HTML tag. It is a custom Kindle/ Mobipocket tag.

<p></p> double spaces paragraphs with first paragraph line indented.

<div></div> double space before and after content within the "division".

 for a line break , <hr> for a horizontal rule, <img> for an image. Note that these three tags do not use end tags, e.g.
 </br> is invalid.

<h1></h1> for

Level 1 Heading

<h2></h2> for

Level 2 Heading

<h3></h3> for

Level 3 Heading

<h4></h4> for

Level 4 Heading

To align a heading in reference to the side of the page you can use the following attribute-value pairs: align="left", align="center", align="right". Headings are aligned by default at left of page with justified text. Unsightly large gap spaces can occur when there are long heading words. Using align attribute-value pairs in the heading tags will change the text to unjustified and eliminate gaps.

<h4 align="center">Centered Example</h4>

<h4 align="center">Right Margin Example</h4>

Paragraphs
"By default, paragraph text is displayed with full justified alignment, and automatic hyphenation. The first line of each paragraph is automatically indented.
Alignment
Readers can adjust the alignment dynamically in the Amazon Kindle wireless reader, and in general we recommend letting readers choose the alignment they prefer, but in some cases you may want to change the alignment to suit your content. You can force your text to be aligned left using the <p align="left"> or <div align="left"> tag.
Indentation
The first line of each paragraph is indented by default. You can change the indentation of the first line of a paragraph using the width attribute:
<p width="N"> (pixels), <p width="N%">,<p width="Nem"> or <p width="Npt">
Note: "N" can represent a positive or negative number.
Examples:
<p width="0"> No indent.
<p width="10%"> Positive indent (10% of page width).
<p width="5em"> Positive indent (5 em).
<p width="-10pt"> Negative indent (10 pt).

<p width="-10"> Negative indent (10 pixels).
For no indent, use <br/> line breaks instead of <p> tags.
Paragraph Spacing
The <p> tag inserts a space before the paragraph. You can adjust spacing using the height attribute:
<p height="N"> (pixels), <p height="N%">, <p height="Nem"> or <p height="Npt"> Note: "N" can represent a positive or negative number.
To avoid the <p> tag's default spacing, use <br /> instead of <p>."

From Amazon DTP >> Support Home >> Formatting Guide >> Advanced HTML Formatting >> Document 27

Images
<img> Placeholder for an image. This is an "open" tag, i.e. not paired.
It must include the attribute-value pair src="URI". e.g. <img src="Kindle.jpg">
See Image Attributes below for examples.

Links
<a> </a> Anchor for hyperlink.
For an external link it requires the attribute-value pair href="URL" , e.g. <a pair href="http://www.amazon.com">Amazon.com</a>.
For an internal link (also called a page 'fragment') it requires the attribute-value pair href="#FRAGMENT" , e.g. <a href="#ch1">Chapter 1</a>.
The fragment must be tagged with either an anchor plus the attribute-value pair name="FRAGMENT" or with the attribute-value pair id="FRAGMENT" inside any other tag, e.g.
<a name="ch1">Chapter 1</a>. or <h3

name="ch1">Chapter 1</h3>.
Fragment values must be unique, e.g. having two
fragments identified as "ch1" will leave the links so
named inoperable.

Lists
<dl> </dl> Creates a definition list of enclosed definitions
<dd> </dd> each followed by an enclosed definition term
<dt> </dt>. Note <dd> is indented, e.g.

> Kindle

The revolutionary eReader from Amazon.com
<ol> </ol> Creates a numbered list from enclosed items,
1. each of which is identified
2. <li> tag.items.</li>

<li> </li> Identifies an item in an ordered (numbered) or
unordered (bullet) list.
<ul> </ul> Creates a bullet list
- from enclosed
- <li> tag.items.</li>

Text
<b></b> for **bold**
<i></i> for *italic*
<font size="N"></font> Example: font size="4"

Some Frequently Used Character Entities
© for © copyright symbol.
  for s p a c e s
— for —
‘ for ', ’ for '
“ for ", ” for "
See a complete list of HTML character entities at
W3Schools.com (use the Entity Name codes—**not** the
Entity Number codes).

Alphabetical List of HTML Tags for Kindle

Reference Amazon DTP >> Support Home >> Formatting Guide >> Advanced HTML Formatting >> Document 30

<!-- --> For enclosing comments that will not be displayed in a browser or the Kindle, e.g. <!-- This is a comment. -->

<a> </a> Anchor for hyperlink.
For an external link it requires the attribute-value pair href="URL" , e.g. <a pair href="http://www.amazon.com">Amazon.com</a>.
For an internal link (also called a page "fragment") it requires the attribute-value pair href="#FRAGMENT" , e.g. <a href="#ch1">Chapter 1</a>. Note, if more than one word is used for an ID value, a hyphen or underscore must connect the words. Spaces within the value quotation marks are illegal.
The fragment must be tagged with either an anchor plus the attribute-value pair name="FRAGMENT" or with the attribute-value pair id="FRAGMENT" inside any other tag, e.g.
<a name="ch1">Chapter 1</a>. or <h3 name="ch1">Chapter 1</h3>.
Fragment values must be unique, e.g. having two fragments identified as "ch1" will leave the links so named inoperable.

<b> </b> Formats enclosed text as **bold**.
It accepts the attribute-value pair id="UNIQUE-NAME".

<big> </big> Increases font size of enclosed text to one point (1/72") larger than the current size.

It accepts the attribute-value pair id="UNIQUE-NAME".

<blockquote> </blockquote> "Sets off long quotes from body text; creates a margin of white space around quoted text, indented on the left-hand side only. You cannot use paragraph tags inside blockquote elements - use the break (br) tag instead. There is no default indentation or spacing for lines inside blockquote elements." — Amazon. Example

Lorem ipsum dolor sit amet, consectetur adipisicing elit, sed do eiusmod tempor incididunt ut labore et dolore magna aliqua. Ut enim ad minim veniam, quis nostrud exercitation ullamco laboris nisi ut aliquip ex ea commodo consequat. Duis aute irure dolor in reprehenderit in voluptate velit esse cillum dolore eu fugiat nulla pariatur. Excepteur sint occaecat cupidatat non proident, sunt in culpa qui officia deserunt mollit anim id est laborum.

> <blockquote>
> The quick brown fox jumped over the lazy dog.
> </blockquote>

Lorem ipsum dolor sit amet, consectetur adipisicing elit, sed do eiusmod tempor incididunt ut labore et dolore magna aliqua. Ut enim ad minim veniam, quis nostrud exercitation ullamco laboris nisi ut aliquip ex ea commodo consequat. Duis aute irure dolor in reprehenderit in voluptate velit esse cillum dolore eu fugiat nulla pariatur. Excepteur sint occaecat cupidatat non proident, sunt in culpa qui officia deserunt mollit anim id est laborum. <body> </body> Encloses the body of the HTML file.

<blockquote> </blockquote> creates a section separated by double spaced lines. Example:
Lorem ipsum dolor sit amet, consectetur adipisicing elit, sed do eiusmod tempor incididunt ut labore et dolore magna aliqua. Ut enim ad minim veniam, quis nostrud exercitation ullamco laboris nisi ut aliquip ex ea commodo consequat. Duis aute irure dolor in reprehenderit in voluptate velit esse cillum dolore eu fugiat nulla pariatur. Excepteur sint occaecat cupidatat non proident, sunt in culpa qui officia deserunt mollit anim id est laborum.

> <blockquote>
> The quick brown fox jumped over the lazy dog.
> </blockquote>

Lorem ipsum dolor sit amet, consectetur adipisicing elit, sed do eiusmod tempor incididunt ut labore et dolore magna aliqua. Ut enim ad minim veniam, quis nostrud exercitation ullamco laboris nisi ut aliquip ex ea commodo consequat. Duis aute irure dolor in reprehenderit in voluptate velit esse cillum dolore eu fugiat nulla pariatur. Excepteur sint occaecat cupidatat non proident, sunt in culpa qui officia deserunt mollit anim id est laborum.

 Creates a line break. This is an "open" tag (not paired, i.e. theris no such tag </br>).

<center> </center> Centers text horizontally, e.g.
Page Center

It accepts the attribute-value pair id="UNIQUE-NAME".

<cite> </cite> Text formatted as *italic*.
. It accepts the attribute-value pair id="UNIQUE-NAME".

<dd> </dd> Encloses the definition of a term in a
definition list (<dl> </dl>). Note it is indented, e.g.
> The Kindle is the revolutionary eReader from
> Amazon.com

It accepts the attribute-value pair id="UNIQUE-NAME",
and
title="TEXT" which creates text in a pop-up box when
readers mouse over this element.

<del> </del> Text is formatted as ~~strike through~~.
It accepts the attribute-value pair id="UNIQUE-NAME".

<dfn> </dfn> Text is formatted as *italic*.
It accepts the attribute-value pair id="UNIQUE-NAME".

<div> </div> Defines a division or section of a document.
It accepts the attribute-value pair align="left", e.g.
this division is at **left margin**.
or the attribute-value pair align="center", e.g.
> this division is at **center** page.
or the attribute-value pair align="right", e.g.
this division is at **right margin**.
and the attribute-value pair id="UNIQUE-NAME" and
bgcolor="COLOR" which defines the background color
for this section.

<em> </em> Text is formatted as *italic*.
It accepts the attribute-value pair id="UNIQUE-NAME".

<font> </font> Determines the appearance of the enclosed

text.

It accepts the attribute-value pair size="N" (N may be a number or number %),

Examples: size="1" size="2" size="3" size="4" size="5" size="6" size="7"

and the attribute-value pair id="UNIQUE-NAME".

<head> </head> Contains information about the HTML document. Should enclose only the <base>, <link>, <meta>, <title>, <style>, and <script> tags. Information enclosed in the tags is not displayed in the final product.

<h1 align="left"> to <h6> Formats enclosed text as a section heading: <h1> (largest) through <h6> (smallest).

<hr> Horizontal "rule" or line to divide sections. This is an "open" tag, i.e. not paired.
It accepts the attribute-value pair color="NAME" (e.g. gray),
the attribute-value pair width="N" (N may be a number or %),
and the attribute-value pair id="UNIQUE-NAME".

<html> </html> Indicates the start and end of an HTML document.
<i> </i> Text is formatted as italic. It accepts the attribute-value pair id="UNIQUE-NAME".

<img> Placeholder for an image. This is an "open" tag, i.e. not paired.

It must include the attribute-value pair src="URI". e.g.
<img src="Kindle.jpg">.
It accepts the attribute-value pairs:
id="UNIQUE-NAME"

Image Attributes

Attribute-Value: border="N" (N=number in pixels).
Example: border="5"

Attribute-Value: align="top" aligns the top of the image
with the top of the current line.
Example:
Lorem ipsum dolor sit amet, consectetur adipisicing elit,
sed do eiusmod tempor incididunt ut labore et dolore
magna aliqua.  Ut enim ad minim

veniam, quis nostrud exercitation ullamco laboris nisi ut
aliquip ex ea commodo consequat. Duis aute irure dolor
in reprehenderit in voluptate velit esse cillum dolore eu

fugiat nulla pariatur. Excepteur sint occaecat cupidatat non proident, sunt in culpa qui officia deserunt mollit anim id est laborum.

Attribute-Value: align="texttop", Effect: Aligns the top the image with the top of the text in the current line. Example:
Lorem ipsum dolor sit amet, consectetur adipisicing elit, sed do eiusmod tempor incididunt ut labore et dolore magna aliqua. Ut enim ad minim

veniam, quis nostrud exercitation ullamco laboris nisi ut aliquip ex ea commodo consequat. Duis aute irure dolor in reprehenderit in voluptate velit esse cillum dolore eu fugiat nulla pariatur. Excepteur sint occaecat cupidatat non proident, sunt in culpa qui officia deserunt mollit anim id est laborum.

Attribute-Value: align="absmiddle", Effect: Centers the image vertically in the current line.
Example:
Lorem ipsum dolor sit amet, consectetur adipisicing elit, sed do eiusmod tempor incididunt ut labore et dolore magna aliqua. Ut enim ad minim veniam, quis nostrud exercitation ullamco laboris nisi ut aliquip ex ea commodo consequat. Duis aute irure dolor in reprehenderit in voluptate velit esse cillum dolore eu fugiat nulla pariatur. Excepteur sint occaecat cupidatat

non proident, sunt in culpa qui officia deserunt mollit

anim id est laborum. Ut enim ad minim veniam, quis nostrud exercitation ullamco laboris nisi ut aliquip ex ea commodo consequat. Duis aute irure dolor in reprehenderit in voluptate velit esse cillum dolore eu fugiat nulla pariatur. Excepteur sint occaecat cupidatat non proident, sunt in culpa qui officia deserunt mollit anim id est laborum.

Attribute-Value: align="middle", Effect: Centers the image vertically in the middle of the text of the current line.
Example:
Lorem ipsum dolor sit amet, consectetur adipisicing elit, sed do eiusmod tempor incididunt ut labore et dolore magna aliqua. Ut enim ad minim veniam, quis nostrud exercitation ullamco laboris nisi ut aliquip ex ea commodo consequat. Duis aute irure dolor in reprehenderit in voluptate velit esse cillum dolore eu fugiat nulla pariatur. Excepteur sint occaecat cupidatat non proident, sunt in culpa qui officia deserunt mollit

anim id est laborum. Ut enim ad minim veniam, quis nostrud exercitation ullamco laboris nisi ut aliquip ex ea commodo consequat. Duis aute irure dolor in reprehenderit in voluptate velit esse cillum dolore eu fugiat nulla pariatur. Excepteur sint occaecat cupidatat non proident, sunt in culpa qui officia deserunt mollit anim id est laborum.

Attribute-Value: align="absbottom", Effect: Align the bottom of the image with the bottom of the current line. Example:
Lorem ipsum dolor sit amet, consectetur adipisicing elit, sed do eiusmod tempor incididunt ut labore et dolore magna aliqua. Ut enim ad minim veniam, quis nostrud exercitation ullamco laboris nisi ut aliquip ex ea commodo consequat. Duis aute irure dolor in reprehenderit in voluptate velit esse cillum dolore eu fugiat nulla pariatur. Excepteur sint occaecat cupidatat non proident, sunt in culpa qui officia deserunt mollit

anim id est laborum. Ut enim ad minim

veniam, quis nostrud exercitation ullamco laboris nisi ut aliquip ex ea commodo consequat. Duis aute irure dolor in reprehenderit in voluptate velit esse cillum dolore eu fugiat nulla pariatur. Excepteur sint occaecat cupidatat non proident, sunt in culpa qui officia deserunt mollit anim id est laborum.

Attribute-Value: align="bottom", Effect: Aligns the bottom of the image with the baseline of the text in the current line.
Example:
Lorem ipsum dolor sit amet, consectetur adipisicing elit, sed do eiusmod tempor incididunt ut labore et dolore magna aliqua. Ut enim ad minim veniam, quis nostrud exercitation ullamco laboris nisi ut aliquip ex ea commodo consequat. Duis aute irure dolor in reprehenderit in voluptate velit esse cillum dolore eu fugiat nulla pariatur. Excepteur sint occaecat cupidatat non proident, sunt in culpa qui officia deserunt mollit anim id est laborum. Ut enim ad minim veniam, quis nostrud exercitation ullamco laboris nisi ut aliquip ex ea commodo consequat. Duis aute irure dolor in reprehenderit in voluptate velit esse cillum dolore eu fugiat nulla pariatur. Excepteur sint occaecat cupidatat non proident, sunt in culpa qui officia deserunt mollit anim id est laborum.

<li> </li> Identifies an item in an ordered (numbered) or unordered (bullet) list.
It accepts the attribute-value pair id="UNIQUE-NAME", and
title="TEXT" which creates text in a pop-up box when readers mouse over this element.

<ol> </ol> Creates a numbered list from enclosed items,
1. each of which is identified
2. by a <li> tag.
It accepts the attribute-value pair id="UNIQUE-NAME".

<p> </p> Defines a paragraph of text with the first line indented; creates a line break at the end of the enclosed text.
Alignment values can be found in the above section titled "Paragraphs".
It accepts the attribute-value pair id="UNIQUE-NAME", and
title="TEXT" which creates text in a pop-up box when readers mouse over this element.

<s> </s> Formats text as ~~strike through~~. See also, <strike>.
It accepts the attribute-value pair id="UNIQUE-NAME", and
title="TEXT" which creates text in a pop-up box when readers mouse over this element.

<small> </small> Text is one point smaller than the current size.
It accepts the attribute-value pair id="UNIQUE-NAME".

<span> </span> Applies defined attributes to in-line text.
It accepts the attribute-value pair bgcolor="COLOR", and

Defines the background color for this element.
title="TEXT" which creates text in a pop-up box when
readers mouse over this element.
Example: <span bgcolor="silver" title="The background
color is Silver."> Mouseover this sentence for a popup
message</span>

<strike> </strike> Formats text as ~~strike through~~. See also,
<s>.
It accepts the attribute-value pair id="UNIQUE-NAME".

<strong> </strong> Formats enclosed text as **bold**. See
also, <b>.
It accepts the attribute-value pair id="UNIQUE-NAME".

 Text as subscript, i.e. a reduced font size
and dropped below the baseline of the text$_a$.
It accepts the attribute-value pair id="UNIQUE-NAME".

 Text as superscript, i.e. a reduced font size
and placed above the baseline, as in a reference to a
footnte[1].
It accepts the attribute-value pair id="UNIQUE-NAME".

<u> </u> Formats enclosed text as <u>underlined</u>.
It accepts the attribute-value pair id="UNIQUE-NAME".

<ul> </ul> Creates a bullet list
- from enclosed
- <li> tag.items.</li>
It accepts the attribute-value pair id="UNIQUE-NAME".

<var> </var> Text formatted as *italic*.

It accepts the attribute-value pair id="UNIQUE-NAME".

Glossary

Acknowledgment
A page where the author thanks individuals and organizations who helped with the book. It is usually part of a book's front matter.

Appendix
A part of a book's back matter listing resources, tables, or other reference material.

Back Matter
The contents of a book that appears after the main text, e.g. afterword, appendix, colophon, glossary, and index.

Bibliography
Part of a book's back matter in which other books or articles are cited as resources.

Bio
A brief description of the author's life and writing experience. It often appears in the back matter, although it may appear in the front matter.

Blurb
A description of an author and/or book content.

Body
The main part of the book not including frnt matter and back matter.

Bold
Type with a **darker** appearance

Caption
Text that refers to refer to an image.

DPI
"Dots per square inch,"; a measure of resolution of

images, printers, and monitors.

Em Dash

A dash used in punctuation the width of one letter "M".

Fair Use

The use of a limited portion of copyrighted material without permission from the copyright owner.

Foreword

Remarks written by someone other than the author. It is placed in the front matter of the book.

Front Matter

The book's pages before the main content e.g. title page, copyright page, contents table, foreword, etc.

Gray Scale

The range of the color gray in shades from white to black..

Introduction

An exposition of the full topic of a book with an explanation of the author's point of view. It may also suggest what the reader's point of view should be. It is placed at the start of the body of the book.

Italic

Type with *sloping letters.*

Joint Photographic Experts Group (JPEG)

The group that created the image file format used for photographs.

Justify

Alignment of text along both margins achieved by adjusting the spacing between the words and characters.

OCR

Optical Character Recognition. Reproducing hardcopy as a digital file.

Orphan

A line of text on its own at the top or bottom of a page.

Point

A typesetting unit of height equaling 1/72 inch.

Portable Network Graphics (PNG)

An image format created to improve upon the Graphics Interchange Format (GIF). PNG is best for images with sharp transitions, e.g. text images and line art.

Preface

An explanation, usually by the author, of how the book came to be, its objective, and the scope of the topic. It is placed in the front matter of the book.

Ragged right

Type that is justified to the left margin and the line lengths vary on the right.

Sans Serif

A typeface that has no serifs (small strokes at the end of main stroke of the character).

Widow

See orphan.

2377192

Made in the USA